Hidden Mysteries and the Bible Official Workbook

SECRETS REVEALED: ALIENS/UFOS, GIANTS,

LARRY OLLISON

Harrison House

Harrison House P.O. Box 310, Shippensburg, PA 17257-0310

This book and all other Harrison House's books are available at Christian bookstores and distributors worldwide.

For Worldwide Distribution.

Reach us on the Internet: www.harrisonhouse.com.

ISBN 13 TP: 9781667508856

ISBN 13 eBook: 9781667508863

CONTENTS

INTRODUCTION

Welcome to the **Hidden Mysteries and the Bible Official Workbook**. This workbook is designed to help you uncover and understand the profound and often hidden messages within the Bible. Through detailed exploration of specific chapters and themes, you will gain a deeper insight into God's Word and how it applies to your life. This introduction will provide an overview of key takeaways from the chapters included and what you can expect to gain from this workbook.

Understanding Heaven, Hell, and Eternity

One of the central themes explored in this workbook is the concept of heaven, hell, and eternity as described in the Bible. The Christian view of heaven is not just a spiritual idea but a real, tangible place. Genesis 1:1 introduces us to the multi-dimensional aspect of heaven, with the Hebrew word for heaven being plural, indicating different areas and dimensions. The New Jerusalem, described in Revelation, is a massive city that will descend from heaven, becoming the eternal home for believers.

This understanding helps us grasp the grandeur and reality of God's promises.

In contrast, hell is depicted as a place of eternal punishment initially created for Satan and his angels but also for those who reject Jesus Christ. Through various Greek words like Hades, Gehenna, and Tartarus, the Bible describes different aspects of hell, emphasizing its seriousness and the need for salvation. Reflecting on these concepts will not only deepen your understanding of eternity but also highlight the importance of your relationship with Jesus Christ.

The Uniqueness of the Hebrew Language

Another significant theme is the mystery and uniqueness of the Hebrew language. The Bible, being the inspired Word of God, uses Hebrew in a way that reveals deep and hidden meanings. Each letter in the Hebrew alphabet has a color, frequency, numeric value, and symbol, making it a multi-dimensional language. For example, the letter Dalet symbolizes a door, and the language itself is encoded with divine messages, proving its divine inspiration.

The precision with which the Hebrew Scriptures have been preserved is remarkable. Scribes meticulously copied the Torah, ensuring no errors by using mathematical formulas and even taking ceremonial baths before writing the name of God. This dedication has kept God's Word unaltered through centuries, allowing us to study and understand its original intent and meaning.

Prophecies and Their Fulfillments

The workbook also explores the prophetic nature of the Bible. For instance, Queen Esther's strange request to hang Haman's already dead sons was seen as a prophecy. In 1946, 10 Nazi war criminals were hanged, fulfilling Esther's prophecy and demonstrating the Bible's accuracy and God's control over history. Hidden codes within the Hebrew Bible often reveal prophecies that become evident only after events unfold, showing the supernatural precision of Scripture.

Jesus as the Word

Understanding Jesus as the Word is another crucial aspect. Jesus refers to Himself as the Alpha and Omega, but in Hebrew, it's the Aleph and the Tav, the first and last letters of the Hebrew alphabet. This means Jesus was there in the beginning with God, creating everything. John 1:1 confirms that Jesus is the Word, existing with God from the start, and through Him, all things were made. This deepens our understanding of Jesus' divine nature and His integral role in creation and salvation.

What You Can Expect

As you work through this workbook, you will:

1. **Gain Deeper Insight into Biblical Concepts**: By exploring themes such as heaven, hell, eternity, and the Hebrew language, you will develop a richer understanding of these complex topics. This knowledge will enhance your spiritual growth and comprehension of God's Word.

2. **Reflect on Personal Beliefs and Actions**: The reflective questions included in each chapter encourage you to think deeply about how these biblical truths apply to your life. You will have the opportunity to examine your beliefs, actions, and relationship with Jesus Christ.

3. **Engage in Practical Application**: The actionable steps provided will help you apply what you've learned in practical ways. By cultivating a deeper

understanding, equipping yourself with knowledge, and engaging in faith-sharing activities, you will strengthen your faith and positively impact those around you.

4. **Experience Personal Transformation**: Through the journaling prompts and reflection, you will experience personal transformation as you align your life more closely with biblical teachings. This process will lead to spiritual growth and a stronger, more resilient faith.

5. **Appreciate the Divine Inspiration of Scripture**: By understanding the meticulous preservation of the Hebrew Scriptures and the hidden codes within the Bible, you will gain a greater appreciation for the divine inspiration and accuracy of God's Word.

~

AFTERWORD

The **Hidden Mysteries and the Bible Official Workbook** is a journey into the depths of God's Word. It is designed to uncover the profound and often hidden messages within the Bible, helping you to grow in faith and understanding. As you explore these themes and apply the lessons to your life, you will discover the richness of Scripture and the incredible plan God has for you. Embrace this journey with an open heart and mind, ready to receive the wisdom and revelation that God has for you.

Welcome to the journey of discovering the hidden mysteries of the Bible. May this workbook be a blessing to you, guiding you into deeper knowledge and a closer relationship with God.

~

HOW TO USE THIS WORKBOOK

Welcome to the **Hidden Mysteries and the Bible Official Workbook**. This guide is designed to help you navigate through the workbook effectively, ensuring you get the most out of each chapter and section. By following these steps, you will gain a deeper understanding of the Bible's profound messages and their applications to your life. Here are ten key points to guide you:

1. Start with the Introduction

Before diving into the chapters, read the introduction thoroughly. It provides an overview of the workbook's purpose and key themes. Understanding the broader context will help you grasp the significance of each chapter as you progress.

2. Read the Bible Verses

Each chapter begins with a word of encouragement and a corresponding Bible verse. These verses are foundational to the chapter's content. Reflect on these verses and consider their relevance to your personal faith journey.

3. Engage with the Chapter Summaries

The chapter summaries provide an in-depth look at the key themes and messages. **Every word contains revelation**. As you read these summaries, take notes on points that stand out to you or that you find particularly meaningful. This will help reinforce your understanding and retention of the material.

4. Reflect on the Key Points

Each chapter includes a section titled "10 Key Points Summary." These points highlight the most important takeaways from the chapter. Reflect on these key points and consider how they apply to your life. This reflection will deepen your understanding and help you internalize the lessons.

5. Answer the Reflective Questions

At the end of each chapter, you will find five reflective questions. These questions are designed to provoke thought and personal introspection. Take your time to answer them honestly and thoughtfully. Writing down your responses can help clarify your thoughts and reveal new insights.

6. Implement the Actionable Steps

Each chapter provides three actionable steps to help you apply what you've learned. These steps include cultivating a deeper understanding, equipping yourself with knowledge, and engaging with others. Implementing these steps will help you put your faith into action and make the lessons practical and relevant to your daily life.

7. Journal Your Thoughts

After reflecting on the chapter and answering the questions, use the journaling prompt provided to write about your thoughts and experiences. Journaling is a powerful tool for self-discovery and spiritual growth. It allows you to process your thoughts and document your journey through the workbook.

8. Take Your Time

This workbook is designed for deep reflection and understanding, so don't rush through it. Take your time with each chapter, allowing yourself to fully engage with the material. The goal is not to finish quickly but to absorb and apply the lessons in a meaningful way.

9. Discuss with Others

If possible, discuss the workbook with a study group or a friend. Sharing insights and discussing different perspectives can enhance your understanding and provide additional support and encouragement. It's often helpful to hear how others interpret and apply the same material.

10. Revisit and Reflect

After completing the workbook, revisit your notes, journal entries, and responses to the reflective questions periodically. Reflection is an ongoing process, and you may discover new insights or see growth in areas where you've applied the workbook's teachings. This continuous engagement will reinforce the lessons and help you maintain your spiritual growth.

Final Thoughts

This workbook is a journey into the depths of God's Word. It's designed to help you uncover the profound and often hidden messages within the Bible. By following these steps and fully engaging with the material, you will gain a deeper understanding of Scripture and how it applies to your life. Embrace this journey with an open heart and mind, ready to receive the wisdom and revelation that God has for you.

Welcome to the journey of discovering the hidden mysteries of the Bible. May this workbook be a blessing to you, guiding you into deeper knowledge and a closer relationship with God.

∽

CHAPTER I

ARE WE ALONE?

In our quest for understanding, remember that God's wisdom surpasses all human knowledge. Trust that He reveals His truths to those who seek Him earnestly.

"For as the heavens are higher than the earth, so are My ways higher than your ways, and My thoughts than your thoughts." - Isaiah 55:9 (NKJV)

In Chapter 1, we start with a profound question that has intrigued humanity for ages: **Are we alone?** This question, posed by Ellie Arroway in the film Contact, is central to our exploration of the universe and our place within it. It drives us to seek answers beyond our immediate perception, pushing the boundaries of our understanding. This question isn't just about finding extraterrestrial life. It's about understanding if there is something greater than ourselves that governs the cosmos.

As we **search for understanding**, we quickly realize that the universe's vastness is almost beyond our comprehension. The immensity of space and the passage of time stretch our minds to their limits. Despite our rapid advancements in knowledge, each discovery seems to unveil even more profound mysteries. This overwhelming pursuit of knowledge is a testament to our innate curiosity and the relentless human spirit that drives us to seek out the unknown.

Reflecting on **advancements in space exploration**, I recall a conversation with a NASA scientist about the Apollo 8 program. The scientist mentioned that, at the time, it would take years to process the data they had already collected. Today, our computing power has exponentially increased, but even now, as recently as 2019, NASA has only begun to study moon rocks collected decades ago. These advancements highlight our incredible progress and the persistent challenges we face in decoding the universe's secrets.

Many people ponder the concept of **intelligent design** when contemplating the universe's complexity. A renowned scientist once shared his belief that the universe's intricacies could not be the result of random chance. While he did not believe in the God depicted in religious texts, he acknowledged that some form of higher intelligence must exist to organize and sustain the cosmos. This idea of a grand design offers a compelling perspective that, despite differing beliefs, many can agree upon: the universe operates under a structured and purposeful order.

The **wisdom of God** surpasses all human understanding, as illustrated through biblical references. Isaiah's words remind us that God's intellect is immeasurable. His ability to measure the waters in the hollow of His hand and weigh mountains on scales speaks to a divine wisdom far beyond our grasp. This humbling comparison emphasizes that our knowledge is limited and finite, whereas God's understanding is boundless and eternal.

A personal story about my daughter underscores our **limited understanding**. When she was four, explaining my complex day involving tax accountants and car repairs would have been futile.

Similarly, our comprehension compared to God's is like a child's understanding of adult responsibilities. Just as my simple explanation sufficed for my daughter, God's revelations to us are tailored to our limited capacity to understand His infinite wisdom.

The **miracle of the Bible** lies in its divine inspiration and seamless compilation over thousands of years by 40 authors. Despite its ancient origins, it remains relevant and coherent, providing a unified theme and purpose. This supernatural quality of the Bible is a testament to its divine origin, serving as a guide and source of truth for believers throughout history and into the present day.

The **Holy Spirit** plays a crucial role in revealing the deep things of God to believers. Through the Spirit, we gain insight into divine mysteries that would otherwise remain hidden. This spiritual connection allows us to tap into a higher understanding, bridging the gap between our finite minds and God's infinite wisdom.

Understanding the **seen and unseen worlds** is essential in comprehending our reality. The Bible teaches that the physical and spiritual realms coexist, with the unseen world often influencing the seen. This dual existence challenges us to look beyond what is visible and acknowledge the spiritual forces at play in our lives and the universe.

Lastly, we must recognize the **infallibility of the Word of God**. The Bible stands as the ultimate source of truth, providing answers to life's mysteries and guiding us in our faith. It is a reliable and authoritative text that has endured through time, offering wisdom and insight to those who seek it. By turning to the Bible, we find clarity and understanding in a world filled with unanswered questions.

In conclusion, Chapter 1 of our study emphasizes the importance of seeking answers to the profound question of whether we are alone in the universe. It encourages us to explore the vastness of the cosmos, recognize the role of intelligent design, and trust in the wisdom and guidance of the Bible and the Holy Spirit. Through this journey, we can gain a deeper understanding of our place in the universe and the divine intelligence that orchestrates all of creation.

REFLECTIVE QUESTIONS

1. How does the vastness of the universe influence your perception of humanity's place in it?
2. What are your thoughts on the idea of intelligent design?
3. In what ways has the Bible provided answers to your own life's mysteries?
4. How do you reconcile scientific discoveries with your faith or belief system?
5. What role does the Holy Spirit play in your understanding of God and the universe?

ACTIONABLE STEPS

- **Cultivate Curiosity**: Engage in regular study: Dedicate time each week to study both scientific discoveries and scriptural insights to deepen your understanding of the universe and God's creation.
- **Equip Yourself with Scripture**: Memorize key verses: Commit to memory scriptures that emphasize God's wisdom and creation, such as Isaiah 40:12-14 and Hebrews 11:3.

- **Engage with the Divine**: Pray for insight: Regularly pray for the Holy Spirit to reveal deeper understanding and wisdom about the mysteries of God and creation.

JOURNALING **Prompt**

Reflect on a time when you felt a profound sense of wonder about the universe. How did that experience shape your view of God and His creation? Write about your thoughts and any insights you gained from that moment.

~

_____

_____

_____

_____

_____

_____

_____

_____

_____

_____

_____

_____

_____

_____

_____

_____

_____

_____

_____

_____

_____

_____

_____

_____

_____

_____

_____

_____
_____
_____
_____
_____
_____
_____
_____
_____
_____
_____
_____
_____
_____
_____
_____
_____
_____
_____
_____
_____
_____
_____
_____
_____
_____
_____
_____
_____
_____

IN THE BEGINNING

"The unchanging nature of God's Word provides a firm foundation in an ever-changing world. Trust in His eternal truth and let it guide you through all aspects of life."

***"Jesus Christ is the same yesterday, today, and forever."* - Hebrews 13:8 (NKJV)**

I grew up in a Christian home where we went to church regularly. From an early age, I was taught to check everything against the Bible, and if the Bible said it, I believed it. Because of this, I've adjusted my theology and views many times to align with the Bible. **It's essential to take the sum of the scriptures and align our thinking and beliefs with them rather than cherry-picking verses to fit our opinions.**

In my studies, I found many views on creation. **Science often seemed to be the standard used to prove or disprove the Bible, but true science and the Bible don't conflict.** The Word of God doesn't change, although our understanding of it can deepen over time. Daniel was told to seal up a scroll until the end of days, and much is being revealed now as we approach those times. **The Holy Spirit, given to the church on Pentecost, reveals scripture and brings to light what was previously hidden.** Scientific facts may change, but the foundational truth of the Word of God remains.

There are two main Christian viewpoints on creation: **Young Earth Creationist and Old Earth Creationist.** Both believe in divine design, but they differ on the timeline. Young Earth Creationists interpret the creation days in Genesis as six 24-hour periods, while Old Earth Creationists see them as longer spans of time. The phrase **"bara elohim" in Hebrew, which means "God created," signifies the involvement of the Trinity— Father, Son, and Holy Spirit—in creation.**

The Bible and other ancient texts mention **multiple heavens, suggesting a complex structure to God's creation.** The universe is vast, with trillions of galaxies, each containing countless stars, highlighting the grandeur of God's creation.

There was **a flood before Adam, different from Noah's flood, caused by Satan's rebellion.** This pre-Adamic flood sets the stage for the re-creation days in Genesis, where God brought order out of chaos. Each day involved separating elements and organizing what already existed, rather than creating from nothing.

Understanding Adam and Eve as real people is crucial for understanding original sin and why Jesus had to die for our sins. Their literal existence is essential for our faith and theology.

REFLECTIVE QUESTIONS

1. How does your personal faith background influence your interpretation of the Bible?
2. In what ways can you ensure your beliefs are aligned with the holistic message of the Bible?
3. How do you reconcile scientific discoveries with your faith in the unchanging Word of God?
4. What are your thoughts on the different interpretations of the creation account in Genesis?
5. Why is it important to understand the role of Adam and Eve in the context of sin and redemption?

ACTIONABLE STEPS

- **Cultivate a Habit of Thorough Bible Study-** Make time regularly to study the Bible deeply. Use commentaries and cross-reference scriptures to get a full understanding of biblical teachings.
- **Equip Yourself with Knowledge of Apologetics-** Learn about Christian apologetics so you can confidently defend your faith and understand how science and scripture harmonize. This knowledge will help you explain your beliefs clearly.
- **Engage in Meaningful Discussions-** Join small group discussions or Bible study groups to explore different viewpoints on creation and other theological topics. Talking with others can provide new insights and support your spiritual growth.

JOURNALING **Prompt**

Reflect on a time when your understanding of a biblical principle changed after deeper study. How did this experience strengthen your faith and your commitment to align your beliefs with the Word of God? Write about the process and the impact it had on your spiritual journey.

~

IN THE BEGINNING

_____

_____

_____

_____

_____

_____

_____

_____

_____

_____

_____

_____

_____

_____

_____

_____

_____

_____

_____

_____

_____

_____

_____

_____

_____

_____

_____

_____

CHAPTER 3
THE WORLD BEFORE
ADAM AND EVE

"The unchanging nature of God's Word provides a firm foundation in an ever-changing world. Trust in His eternal truth and let it guide you through all aspects of life."

"Jesus Christ is the same yesterday, today, and forever." - **Hebrews 13:8 (NKJV)**

Before we talk about the world before Adam and Eve, I want to make one thing clear. **Your belief or unbelief about a pre-Adamic civilization does not affect your salvation.** Eternal life is determined by your faith in Jesus Christ, not your views on creation. It's important to keep unity and love within the body of Christ, no matter our differing opinions on this topic.

Scientists believe the universe began from a singularity smaller than an atom, which expanded faster than the speed of light. They estimate the universe is 94 billion light years across and about 13.8 billion years old. These numbers have changed over time and may continue to change with new discoveries.

The launch of telescopes like the Hubble in 1990 and the James Webb Telescope in 2021 has changed our understanding of the universe. **These telescopes let us see farther into space, discovering trillions of stars and billions of galaxies, showing us the vastness of God's creation.**

Genesis 1:1-2 says God created the heavens and the earth perfectly. Isaiah 45:18 confirms that God did not create the earth in vain, meaning it was originally perfect. But something catastrophic happened between Genesis 1:1 and 1:2, making the earth formless and void.

The Bible describes Lucifer as a perfect creation until iniquity was found in him. His rebellion against God, along with a third of the angels, led to his fall from heaven. This caused chaos and destruction on earth, making it formless and void.

Lucifer's fall led to the first flood, submerging the earth in water and making it formless and void. This flood, different from Noah's flood, destroyed the kingdoms and creatures on earth at that time. This catastrophic event marked the end of a previous creation era.

Time was created by God, as stated in Titus 1:2, where God made promises before time began. This means that time is a created thing and that God's existence goes beyond time, being eternal and without beginning.

Ezekiel 28:12-15 describes Lucifer's perfection and fall. The passage uses symbolic language to show Lucifer's beauty, wisdom, and eventual corruption, comparing the fall of the king of Tyre with Satan's fall.

Jeremiah 4:23-26 talks about a time when the earth was formless and void, with no light and trembling mountains. This vision shows a pre-Adamic destruction caused by Lucifer's rebellion, making the earth desolate and chaotic.

The Bible talks about two significant floods: the Luciferian flood, caused by Lucifer's rebellion, and Noah's

flood, caused by human and angelic sin. The first flood destroyed the earth, making it formless and void, while the second flood destroyed all living flesh but left the earth intact.

In summary, understanding the world before Adam and Eve gives us insight into the events that led to the current state of creation. **Lucifer's rebellion and the destruction of the earth show the consequences of sin and the power of God's redemption.** This perspective helps us appreciate God's plan and the importance of our faith in Jesus Christ.

REFLECTIVE QUESTIONS

1. How does your belief or unbelief in a pre-Adamic civilization impact your understanding of the Bible and creation?
2. What is your perspective on the scientific explanation of the universe's creation?
3. How do advancements in astronomy, such as the Hubble and James Webb Telescopes, enhance your perception of God's creation?
4. What lessons can you learn from Lucifer's rebellion and fall?
5. How do you reconcile the biblical account of two significant floods with your understanding of God's plan for creation?

Actionable Steps

- **Cultivate Unity in Diversity**- Embrace diverse beliefs within the Christian community while focusing on the core belief in Jesus Christ as Lord and

Savior. Promote unity and love among fellow
believers.

- **Equip Yourself with Scientific Knowledge**- Stay
  informed about scientific discoveries and
  advancements in astronomy. Understand how these
  findings can coexist with and enhance your faith.
- **Engage in Biblical Study of Creation**- Study the
  Bible thoroughly, focusing on passages related to
  creation, Lucifer's fall, and the two floods. Use
  commentaries and scholarly resources to deepen
  your understanding.

Journaling Prompt

Reflect on how your understanding of creation has evolved
over time. How have scientific discoveries and biblical study
shaped your beliefs? Write about the impact this has had on your
faith and how you reconcile different viewpoints with your trust
in God's Word.

∾

THE WORLD BEFORE ADAM AND EVE

_____

_____

_____

_____

_____

_____

_____

_____

_____

_____

_____

_____

_____

_____

_____

_____

_____

_____

_____

_____

_____

_____

_____

_____

CHAPTER 4

THE WATCHERS AND THE NEPHILIM

"Even in the most confusing and bizarre events, God's love and purpose shine through. Trust that His plans are always for your ultimate good."

"For I know the thoughts that I think toward you, says the LORD, thoughts of peace and not of evil, to give you a future and a hope." - Jeremiah 29:11 (NKJV)

In Genesis, there's an event that's often misunderstood and ignored by many in the church because it's so strange and hard to comprehend. This event, combined with human perversion, led to the flood in Noah's days:

"Now it came to pass, when men began to multiply on the face of the earth, and daughters were born to them, that the sons of God saw the daughters of men, that they were beautiful; and they took wives for themselves of all whom they chose. ...There were giants on the earth in those days, and also afterward, when the sons of God came in to the daughters of men and they bore children to them. Those were the mighty men (giants) who were of old, men of renown" (Genesis 6:1-2,4).

The "sons of God" who took human wives and had children with them were angels. This is supported by many ancient writings, including the Book of Enoch, the Genesis Apocryphon, the Damascus Document, the Book of Jubilees, the Testament of Reuben, Second Barak, Josephus, and the Septuagint. Even the books of Jude and Second Peter in the Bible agree with this interpretation.

Job provides proof that the sons of God are angels. Some scholars claim Job was mythical, but Ezekiel 14:14 confirms Job was real, placing him alongside Noah and Daniel. Job 38:6-7 describes the sons of God (angels) present at creation, existing before the earth and watching as God created man.

Historically, the oldest interpretation is that the sons of God were angels who had sexual relations with human women, producing giants called the Nephilim. **This view was supported by early church leaders and ancient writers.** The Sethite view, which emerged later, claims the sons of God were descendants of Seth and the daughters of men were descendants of Cain. However, this view is logically and genetically flawed.

In the New Testament, "sons of God" refers to born-again believers. In the Old Testament, the term refers to angels. The angels who sinned before mankind's creation were judged and cast to earth. Hell was created to contain Satan and his angels for eternity (Matthew 25:41). However, a second group of angels, the Watchers, sinned by taking human wives and producing Nephilim. These Watchers are imprisoned in Tartarus until judgment.

Watchers are angels assigned to watch over humanity. Despite the sin of the 200 Watchers, countless other angels remained loyal to God. The Book of Enoch provides detailed accounts of these Watchers and their fall. These angels did not just fall into sin; they deliberately chose to take human wives, fully aware of the consequences.

The giants, or Nephilim, were the offspring of these unions. They consumed the earth's produce and resorted to cannibalism. Perversion on earth included creating hybrids, further corrupting God's creation. These actions contaminated human DNA, posing a threat to the perfect sacrifice required for redemption.

Noah's flood was necessary to eliminate this corruption. Noah was morally and genetically pure, and the flood eradicated the hybrid DNA from the earth. The Watchers were imprisoned for their actions, awaiting final judgment.

Giants reappeared after the flood, but how did this happen? Theories include a second incursion of angels or that Ham's wife carried Nephilim DNA. Giants like Goliath descended from these post-flood Nephilim. The Israelites encountered and fought these giants during their conquest of the Promised Land.

God's plan included purging the corrupted DNA from the earth. Commands to utterly destroy certain tribes were necessary to eliminate the Nephilim. Ultimately, God's interventions, including the flood, were acts of love to preserve humanity and ensure the coming of the perfect sacrifice, Jesus Christ.

REFLECTIVE QUESTIONS

1. How does the account of the Watchers and the Nephilim challenge or confirm your understanding of biblical history?
2. What does the persistence of giants after the flood suggest about the nature of evil and God's intervention?

3. How can the concept of contaminated DNA relate to the importance of purity and holiness in your life?
4. Why do you think God chose to act so decisively with the flood, and what does this tell you about His character?
5. How does understanding the history of the Watchers and Nephilim enhance your appreciation of Jesus' sacrifice?

Actionable Steps

- **Cultivate Awareness of Spiritual Realities-** Acknowledge the spiritual battles and histories that shape our world. Stay vigilant in prayer and study to understand these deeper truths.
- **Equip Yourself with Biblical Knowledge-** Dive into scripture and related ancient texts to gain a fuller understanding of God's plan and the forces at work. Use commentaries and scholarly resources to guide your study.
- **Engage in Holiness and Purity-** Strive to maintain moral and spiritual purity in your life. Recognize the importance of living a life that reflects God's holiness and His call to righteousness.

Journaling Prompt

Reflect on the story of the Watchers and the Nephilim. How does this narrative shape your understanding of God's actions and His plans for humanity? Write about how this deeper insight affects your faith and your daily walk with God.

CHAPTER 5

WHO BUILT THE ANCIENT STRUCTURES?

"In every stone, in every massive structure, there is a reminder of the greatness of God's creation. He is the ultimate architect, and His wonders never cease to amaze us."

The heavens declare the glory of God; and the firmament shows His handiwork. - Psalm 19:1 (NKJV)

A ll around the world, there are ancient structures built with such precision that modern man cannot explain how they were constructed without advanced technology. Many of these structures could not even be duplicated with today's machinery. **Who built these ancient structures?** How were they able to cut the stones, often hard granite, with such razor-sharp precision? Where did they get the mathematical, scientific, and cosmic knowledge and skills required? How did they move the massive megalithic stones that often came from quarries miles away?

First, we must understand that all ancient structures discovered and examined by archaeologists were not built in the same time period. Without understanding who was on earth during their construction, it is difficult to determine who the builders were. Let's look at some of these mysterious structures.

MYSTERIOUS STRUCTURES

The island of Malta played a vital strategic role in World War II as a base for the Allied Powers. Centuries before that, it was home to the Knights Templar, who built enormous fortresses and temples that still stand today. But millennia before all of this, other ancient temples and structures reveal a past inhabited by a civilization with immense strength and access to beings with higher intellect and skills. One such structure is the Hal Saflieni Hypogeum.

THE HYPOGEUM

On one of my trips to Malta with my friends L.A. Marzulli and Bob Ulrich, we explored the Hypogeum, now overseen by UNESCO. Before entering, we had to lock away all communication devices, lights, and cameras. Only one group of ten people is allowed to enter at a time, usually requiring a wait of several months. Thanks to a personal contact in Malta, we were given special entry.

The word "hypogeum" means "underground" in Greek. The Hypogeum was accidentally discovered in 1902 while workers were cutting a cistern for a new housing development. Excavation began in 1903, revealing a large underground palace hewn from solid stone, containing thousands of skeletons, some with elongated skulls. **For some unknown reason, the contents were discarded without being properly cataloged.**

Excavations continued, and in 1908 visitors were allowed to observe the ongoing discoveries. It is estimated the Hypogeum was in use at least 6,000 years ago. The lower main chamber, called "The Holy of Holies," is illuminated during the winter solstice when light comes through its original opening above. There is also an "Oracle Room" with acoustics studied by scientists in 2014. A normal voice spoken from a certain place in the Oracle Room can be heard throughout the Hypogeum. When Bob, L.A., and I stood in that place and spoke, **our voices carried throughout the massive underground palace.** Interestingly, women's voices do not carry the same way.

There are many other interesting details and numerous artifacts discovered in the Hypogeum, but detailing all would require more than a section in a book. However, I recount a historical event concerning the Hypogeum to give a true feeling of its massiveness.

THE LOST STUDENTS

Many years ago, before the lower level was sealed, a teacher and her 30 students entered the underground palace for a field trip. It was reported that there were several overlapping layers of tunnels, allowing travel across the country and even under the Mediterranean Sea to Rome. In the 16th century, knights built fortifications over broken passageways and blocked doorways.

The August 1940 issue of National Geographic magazine tells the story of students being lost in the massive network of tunnels. They were never found. Here's an excerpt from that article:

"While we cycled homeward, our friends told us that the island was honeycombed with a network of underground passages many of them catacombs. Years ago we could walk underground from one end of Malta to the other, but all entrances were closed by the Government because of a tragedy. On a sightseeing trip, comparable to a nature study tour in our own schools, a number of elementary school children

*and their teachers descended into the tunneled maze and did not
return. For weeks, mothers declared that they had heard wailing and
screaming from underground. But numerous excavations and
searching parties brought no trace of the lost souls. After three weeks
they were finally given up for dead."*

As an eyewitness to the Hypogeum and the ancient temples
of the giants on Malta and Gozo, I can testify that these ancient
structures hold many secrets that the natural human cannot
comprehend. Who were these ancient people who numbered in
the tens of thousands and lived completely underground in a
series of hewn-from-stone tunnels and palaces? Where are the
giants who occupied the temples scattered above ground
throughout Malta?

How do we explain the ancient "railway lines" carved into
solid rock, stretching from one end of the island to the other?
These lines are estimated to be at least 7,000 years old, possibly
older. If Adam left the Garden of Eden in 4004 BC as the Bible
says, how could a civilization exist at least 1,000 years before
that? Many artifacts discovered in Malta date back tens of thousands of years earlier.

If this dating is correct, the structures must have been built
by angels and non-humans before Adam left the Garden. How do
we explain the skeletons found? A future civilization could
occupy a previously built structure. **Structures built pre-Adam
and pre-flood could be occupied by post-flood humans.** Stone
structures would not necessarily be destroyed by floodwaters.

SECOND OLDEST TEMPLE ON THE PLANET—ĠGANTIJA

Malta is home to many fascinating archaeological discoveries.
Ġgantija, the second oldest temple and man-made structure
found anywhere on the planet, is located in Malta. This megalithic complex is thought to have been erected as far back as

3600 BC, predating the flood of Noah by many centuries. By biblical chronology, Adam would have been about 400 years old at the time of its construction.

It is thought to be a place of ritual significance. Some of the stones used to build the complex are massive, measuring five meters (about 16 feet) in height and weighing as much as 50 tons. Archaeologists and engineers cannot explain how an early agricultural society, equipped with only stone tools, could have moved the massive megalithic stones.

While there, I asked one of the guides how the stones were moved, and his reply was almost humorous. He pointed to a group of round stones about one foot in diameter scattered around the temple. He claimed the huge megalithic stones were rolled on these small stone balls. Given the long distance the stones were moved, their massive weight, the rough terrain, and the fact that the small round stones would have been crushed, the answer seemed to be the politically correct, talking-point answer required by the governing authority (UNESCO).

Residents have a legend passed through generations that gives another explanation. **The legend says the temple was dedicated to a goddess named Sansuna, a giantess who bore a child to one of the local men.** She built Ġgantija, carrying huge stones 4 kilometers (about 3 miles) from the town of Ta' Cenc, placing them at Ġgantija, "The Place of Giants," in a single day, transporting the stones on her head while holding her half-giant, half-human baby over her shoulder.

A second legend suggests the structure served as a defensive tower built by giants. Either way, the folklore involves giants of enormous size and strength.

GÖBEKLI TEPE

Göbekli Tepe is a Neolithic site in southeastern Türkiye. The site is marked by layers of carved megaliths, estimated to have been constructed in approximately 10000 BC. At Göbekli Tepe, T-shaped limestone megaliths, some more than 16 feet (five meters) high and weighing up to 50 tons, are arranged in circular formations. Some megaliths are carved with elaborate designs featuring foxes, lions, scorpions, and other images. Although Göbekli Tepe predates Stonehenge by 6,000 years, it was not seriously investigated until the 1990s. Most experts identify it as a ritual site. How did a hunting, agricultural prehistoric tribe move, carve, and strategically place the massive monoliths? Did they have help from fallen angels? If this structure was in use 12,000 years ago, it predates Adam and Eve by 6,000 years.

THE SPHINX OF GIZA

The Sphinx of Giza is one of the most mysterious construction projects in the world. It is over 60 feet in height, 240 feet in length, and hewn from one stone. Located on the Giza Plateau, 10 kilometers (6 miles) west of Cairo, Egypt, it is near the three great pyramids of Khufu, Khafre, and Menkaure. Estimated to have been constructed sometime between 5000 BC to 8000 BC, it possibly predates Adam and was not built by man. Who could have built the sphinx?

THE PYRAMIDS OF EGYPT

The great pyramids of Egypt have baffled archaeologists and the scientific community for centuries. Over 118 pyramids have been discovered in Egypt, with more yet to be found. Their construction defies logic. Modern engineers and geologists have been unable to determine how the ancient builders designed the foundations. **Modern buildings settle at a rate of 6 inches per 100 years.** The US Capitol Building has settled over 5 inches since its construction in 1793, yet the Great Pyramid has only settled one-half inch in over 5,000 years. The blocks used in its construction weigh approximately 6 million tons.

How did the ancients understand geology and engineering better than modern engineers? The Great Pyramid is constructed with 2.25 million blocks, each cut, transported, and assembled with razor-like precision, leaving only 2/100ths of an inch spacing between the stones.

Traditional teaching says the Great Pyramid was constructed in 20 years, meaning each stone had to be quarried, transported, cut to precision, and put into place in less than five minutes, which seems impossible. In 1940, a British Air Force pilot discovered it had eight sides instead of four. At dawn and sunset during the spring and autumn equinox, the eight sides can be clearly seen from the air, requiring extremely precise alignment millennia ago. **Did the ancients have greater knowledge of geology and science, or were they assisted by more advanced beings?**

NEWGRANGE

Newgrange is located in the Boyne Valley of Ireland. It is a 5,200-year-old passage tomb built by Stone Age farmers. The mound covers an area of one acre, about 43 feet high, and 279 feet in diameter. A passage of 62 feet leads to a chamber with three alcoves, encircled by 97 engraved monoliths called kerbstones. The construction date is estimated at 3200 BC, possibly older than Stonehenge and the Giza Pyramids.

Newgrange is enriched with megalithic art and is known as

the jewel in the crown of Ireland's Ancient East. It is a colossal house of astronomical significance. The alignment within the chamber creates illumination with the rising sun in the winter solstice, lasting for about 17 minutes. This makes Newgrange the most accurate time-telling device of that time.

How could an agrarian society with stone and wood tools accomplish this? Did they have help? The Book of Enoch tells us the Watchers taught men the knowledge of the planets, stars, and constellations. **Enoch 8:3 says, "Semyaza taught enchantments, and root-cuttings. Armaros taught how to resolve enchantments. Barakel taught astrology. Kokabel taught the constellations (signs). Temel taught the knowledge of the clouds (astrology). Asradel taught the courses of the moon."**

Could the ancient people have received their knowledge from the Watchers? Could their advanced knowledge and assistance from the Watchers and giants have enabled them to move the massive intricately hewn stones and guide the precise solstice alignments? The Bible and ancient writings do not contradict this possibility.

THE TOWER OF BABEL

After the flood, God commanded Noah and his sons to "Be fruitful, and multiply, and replenish the earth" (Genesis 9:1). However, their descendants settled in Babylonia, speaking one language. They said to each other, "Come, let's build a great city for ourselves with a tower that reaches into the sky. This will make us famous and keep us from being scattered all over the world" (Genesis 11:4).

Because they put their faith in themselves rather than God, God confused their language, stopping construction, and they were dispersed. **"And the Lord said, Behold, they are one people and they have all one language; and this is only the**

beginning of what they will do, and now nothing they have imagined they can do will be impossible for them" (Genesis 11:6).

This sounds similar to Lucifer's attempt after the original creation. Because Lucifer attempted to ascend into the heavens, he was cast to the earth. Likewise, the builders of Babel attempted to reach the heavens but were dispersed. In both cases, pride was their downfall.

BIBLE TIMELINE OF PERIODS OF CIVILIZATIONS

- **Original Creation (Genesis 1:1) until the Luciferian Flood (Genesis 1:2):** Civilizations of angels and possibly nonhuman beings existed on earth. Lucifer ruled and rebelled, leading to the earth being covered in water and destroyed.
- **From the Re-Creation to the Sin of Adam:** This period ended near 4004 BC. Adam and Eve were in the Garden, and there may have been nonhuman beings outside the Garden.
- **After Adam Left the Garden (4004 BC) and Before the Flood of Noah (2348 BC):** During this 1,656-year period, humans, Watchers, fallen angels, and giants (Nephilim) existed.
- **After the Flood of Noah (2348 BC) Until the Resurrection of Jesus:** Humans, angels of God, fallen angels, and Nephilim existed until they were eliminated by Israel's armies.
- **From the Resurrection of Jesus Until Today:** This period is the age of grace, the church age, and the last days. Born-again believers are called the sons of God, with authority over the enemy. Humans, fallen

angels, the Holy Spirit, and angels of God are on earth.

SUMMARY

After the original creation, there was a civilization on earth with kings, kingdoms, and commerce (Ezekiel 28:16; Isaiah 14:12). Lucifer was involved in trading with them. They may have been angelic and/or physical nonhuman beings, not human since Adam was the first man (1 Corinthians 15:45,47). **We do not know how long this civilization existed before Lucifer's fall, but there were great structures built.**

God, in His grace and mercy, restored the earth, created man, and placed him in the Garden. We are not told how long Adam lived in the Garden before his sin, but the genealogy of Jesus traces back to Adam, showing Adam left the Garden 4,000 years before Jesus' birth.

After Adam left the Garden, there was great sin and perversion, but God cleansed the earth with a flood at Noah's time, approximately 4,400 years ago. **So, who built the ancient structures and how?** If built after Noah's flood, humans with available tools built them, possibly assisted by Nephilim. If built after Adam left the Garden but before Noah's flood, they could have been built by Watchers, giants, humans, or a combination. If over 6,000 years old, they were obviously built before Adam left the Garden, possibly during the time of ancient civilizations of nonhuman beings and angels before the earth was covered by water in Genesis 1:2.

A deep study of Scripture reveals the truth. Sometimes this requires unlearning previous beliefs to understand the ultimate truth revealed in God's Word.

1. What role do you think advanced beings, such as angels or giants, played in the construction of ancient structures?
2. How does understanding the possible builders of these structures change your perception of human history?
3. What lessons can we learn from the civilizations that built these ancient structures?
4. How does the Bible's account of creation and the flood help explain the existence of these ancient structures?
5. In what ways can our faith be strengthened by exploring the mysteries of these ancient structures?

Actionable Steps

- **Cultivate** a deeper understanding of biblical history by studying the accounts of creation, the flood, and the giants. This will help you connect the dots between ancient structures and biblical events.
- **Equip** yourself with knowledge from various sources, including archaeological findings, ancient texts, and modern research. This will provide a well-rounded perspective on the mysteries of ancient structures.
- **Engage** in discussions with others about the possible connections between ancient structures and biblical events. Sharing your insights can help others see the Bible's relevance to historical and archaeological discoveries.

JOURNALING **Prompt**

Reflect on a time when you encountered something that seemed impossible to explain. How did this experience challenge or strengthen your faith? Write about how exploring the mysteries of ancient structures can deepen your understanding of God's creation and His plans for humanity.

∾

CHAPTER 6
ANGELS OF GOD

God's angels are always around us, protecting and guiding us
even when we cannot see them. Trust that God has sent His
angels to watch over you.

**"For He shall give His angels charge over you, to keep you in
all your ways." - Psalm 91:11 (NKJV)**

Any discussion of the spirit world wouldn't be complete
without exploring angels. Due to ancient fables, cult
teachings, and Hollywood's fictional scripts, the accurate teaching about angels has been skewed. There are thousands of writings about angels, but the ultimate authority is the
Holy Bible. Let's uncover the mystery of angels based on biblical
accounts.

- **The Creation of Angels**: Before creating man, God
  made angels—magnificent, glorious creatures filled
  with beauty. There are different ranks among angels,
  such as archangels, seraphim, cherubim, living

creatures, and other heavenly hosts. All angels once honored God with praise and worship. They were present when God created man on Day 6. Psalm 8 shows the angels expressing awe at God's creation of man, highlighting that man was created a little lower than God (Elohim) and not the angels.

- **Angels have a purpose**: Angels were never meant to be like God. They were created with specific functions and were not to mix with humans. God's creation must stay within their domain. The Greek word "angelos" means "messenger." Throughout history, God has used angels to deliver messages, like Gabriel delivering messages to Zechariah, Mary, and Joseph.

- **When Were Angels Created?**: Angels haven't always existed. Ezekiel 28:15 tells us Lucifer was perfect on the day he was created, indicating that angels were created at a specific time. The exact date is unknown, but it was during the creation of the heavens and the earth. Initially, all angels were good. They were created perfect, just like the heavens and the earth.

- **Two Groups of Angels**: Today, there are two groups of angels on earth. The first group consists of God's angels who stayed loyal and didn't sin. They are messengers of God and minister to those who will inherit salvation. The second group consists of fallen angels who followed Lucifer. They are now evil spirits and are restricted from God's presence. There's also a third group, the Watchers, imprisoned in Tartarus until the day of judgment.

- **The Power of Angels Demonstrated**: Throughout history, God has sent angels to intervene in human affairs. Angels can move between the unseen and our physical world, altering their appearance and changing the laws of physics. Examples include an angel killing 185,000 Assyrian soldiers in response to King Hezekiah's prayer and the unseen angelic armies protecting Elisha and his servant.

- **Angels Inflict Blindness**: When two angels were sent to Sodom, the men of the city surrounded Lot's house, demanding to see the angels. The angels struck the men with blindness, demonstrating their power to protect and intervene.
- **The Fourth Man in the Fiery Furnace**: Shadrach, Meshach, and Abed-Nego refused to worship Nebuchadnezzar's golden statue and were thrown into a fiery furnace. An angel, described as the "Son of God," appeared in the furnace, protecting them from harm.
- **Angels Guarding the Tree of Life**: After Adam's sin, God placed cherubim with a flaming sword to guard the way to the tree of life, preventing fallen man from accessing eternal life.
- **Angel Detained for Twenty-One Days**: Daniel's prayer was heard, and an angel was dispatched but delayed for 21 days by the spirit prince of Persia. Michael the archangel intervened, highlighting the spiritual battles that occur in the unseen realm.
- **Ezekiel's Encounter with Living Creatures**: Ezekiel's vision of living creatures with multiple faces and wings, moving as the spirit directed, shows the diversity and purpose of angels in delivering messages from God.
- **Angels Shut the Lions' Mouths**: Daniel was thrown into the lions' den but survived because an angel shut the lions' mouths, protecting him.

- **Angel Gabriel Visits Zechariah and Mary**: Gabriel delivered messages to Zechariah about the birth of John the Baptist and to Mary about the birth of Jesus, emphasizing angels' role as messengers of significant events.
- **Angels Praise God at Jesus' Birth**: Angels praised God at the announcement of Jesus' birth, showing their role in worship and proclamation.
- **Peter Rescued from Prison**: An angel rescued Peter from prison, illustrating angels' ability to intervene in impossible situations.
- **Angel Appears to Paul**: Paul experienced angelic visitations, receiving guidance and knowledge of future events, showing that angels can bring divine messages and support.
- **Three Angels During the Great Tribulation**: During the Great Tribulation, three angels will preach the gospel, proclaim the defeat of Babylon, and warn against taking the mark of the beast, demonstrating God's continued desire for salvation.
- **Angels Worship in Heaven**: The throne room of God is surrounded by angels worshiping Him, highlighting their eternal role in praising and serving God.

REFLECTIVE QUESTIONS

1. What role do you believe angels play in your daily life?
2. How can understanding the biblical accounts of angels strengthen your faith?

3. In what ways have you experienced or witnessed angelic intervention?
4. What lessons can we learn from the angels' obedience and dedication to God?
5. How can you apply the knowledge of angels' protection and guidance in your prayer life?

Actionable Steps

- **Cultivate** a habit of acknowledging God's angels in your prayers, thanking Him for their protection and guidance.
- **Equip** yourself with biblical knowledge about angels by studying the scriptures mentioned in this chapter, enhancing your understanding of their roles.
- **Engage** in conversations with fellow believers about the reality and significance of angels, sharing insights and experiences to encourage one another.

Journaling Prompt

Reflect on a time when you felt protected or guided in an extraordinary way. How did this experience impact your faith? Write about how understanding the presence and purpose of angels can deepen your trust in God's divine plan for your life.

~

CHAPTER 7

UFOS AND THE BIBLE

Even in the face of strange and unexplained phenomena, remember that God has given us a spirit of power, love, and a sound mind. We can trust in His protection and stand firm in our faith.

"For God has not given us a spirit of fear, but of power and of love and of a sound mind." - 2 Timothy 1:7 (NKJV)

F or centuries, people have been fascinated by unidentified flying objects (UFOs) and extraterrestrial life. This interest was first captured in the 1902 film "A Trip to the Moon." Since then, numerous movies have depicted space travel and aliens, contributing to our fascination with the unknown. In 2021, the U.S. government began releasing reports on UFOs, revealing that **these objects can move at incredible speeds**, far beyond human capabilities. This has made what was once considered fantasy a serious topic of discussion among scientists and political leaders.

The term "UFO" was coined by the U.S. Air Force in 1952, following a sighting near Mount Rainier in 1947. However, due to the stigma associated with the term, it has been replaced by "UAP" (Unidentified Anomalous Phenomena). The U.S. government has disclosed numerous military and commercial pilot encounters with UFOs, supported by videos from the Pentagon. NASA has also prioritized the search for extraterrestrial life, although **no credible evidence has been found so far**.

Movies and media have desensitized the public to the idea of aliens, often portraying them as wise and benevolent beings. However, some people claim to communicate with aliens through various means, but these are actually demonic spirits trying to deceive. **The Bible warns against contacting such spirits**, which are fallen angels. We need to use the gift of discerning spirits to tell the difference between truth and deception.

Reports of UFO sightings and encounters raise questions about the nature of these beings. Some may represent God, while others are part of the principalities and powers of darkness. **The Bible describes a spiritual battle against these forces**. Therefore, we must be cautious and discerning.

The Bible contains accounts of unidentified objects and strange encounters. For example, **Ezekiel saw a "wheel within a wheel,"** and Zechariah saw a flying scroll. These could be interpreted as encounters with unidentified objects. The Bible also describes chariots of fire, which might be seen as divine technology used by angels.

Satan often imitates God's work with counterfeit versions. For example, **Moses saw the pattern of the heavenly tabernacle** and built an earthly version. Similarly, Satan creates false religions and counterfeit miracles to deceive people. We need to study the Word of God to recognize these deceptions and not be led astray.

We should not fear these phenomena. **The Bible tells us that God has not given us a spirit of fear,** but of power, love, and a sound mind. If we encounter something strange, we should rebuke it in the name of Jesus. Faith and fear are opposites, and we must choose to operate in faith, trusting in God's protection.

Do UFOs exist? Yes, there is evidence that they do. But you have not been given a spirit of fear, so do not respond to fear. When you hear words of terror and disaster, do not fear. **Remember Psalm 91:7.** Speak it and let it become rhema in your heart: "A thousand may fall at your side, and ten thousand at your right hand; but it shall not come near you."

Why Are They Doing What They're Doing? To summarize, **the players that are on earth right now are the angels of God,** the fallen angels (demons), Satan, mankind, the church, and, of course, the Holy Spirit. So who is orchestrating the manifestations of unidentified objects flying in the atmosphere and into the oceans of the earth?

Since the Roswell incident, the secular world has been pushing the concept that UFOs are alien entities from outer space or other dimensions. It has even been suggested that in the ancient past, the earth was seeded with humans and the aliens have been periodically returning to inspect the progress. **It has been proposed by some that the reported abductions of humans by the aliens are merely physical inspections of the progress of mankind.**

Why would the secular world promote this? Could the underlying reason be the enemy wants to have an explanation ready to implement when the church is caught up and taken to heaven as prophesied in 1 Thessalonians 4:16? In order to keep those remaining on the earth after the rapture under his control, there must be an explanation for this mass abduction. **Could his excuse simply be that it was aliens instead of Jesus?**

UFOs of the Future: It is prophesied in the Bible that in the end of days it would be as in the days of Noah (Luke 17:26). We know that in the days of Noah there was great evil on the earth perpetrated by the forces of darkness. That can be expected as we approach the time of the return of Jesus. But likewise, it is prophesied that in the end of days there will be signs and wonders in the heavens.

"I will show wonders in heaven above and signs in the earth beneath: blood and fire and vapor of smoke" (Acts 2:19). For the person living in this dispensation at the close of the end of days, great discernment must be exercised. As God performs wonders, likewise Satan attempts to imitate them making himself seem benevolent.

When Moses threw down his staff and it became a serpent, Pharaoh's magicians also threw down their staffs, which also became serpents. **Satan cannot create anything; he only attempts to duplicate with deception.** Living in the end of days we must clearly discern whether the things we see are like the serpent of Moses or the serpent of Pharaoh's magicians. Remember, on the floor they all looked the same, but they weren't. The staff that became a serpent when Moses threw it to the ground swallowed the serpents of the magicians.

"For false christs and false prophets will rise and show great signs and wonders to deceive, if possible, even the elect" (Matthew 24:24). Do not be led astray by what looks right—be led by discerning of spirits furnished by the Holy Spirit so you will know the truth and not be led into deception. **Remember, it's not what you see that sets you free, it's knowing the truth that sets you free** (John 8:32). So when it comes to seeing something in the sky that you cannot identify, always remember that the fallen angels are not the only ones at work in the end of days; angels of God are traveling through portals back and forth from heaven doing the work of God on the earth (John 1:51).

. . .

Reflective Questions

1. What do you believe is the significance of the government's recent disclosures about UFOs?
2. How can understanding the biblical perspective on UFOs help you address questions from others?
3. In what ways have movies and media influenced your perception of extraterrestrial life?
4. Why is it important for Christians to discern the spirits behind these phenomena?
5. How can you strengthen your faith to overcome fear related to unknown phenomena like UFOs?

Actionable Steps

- **Cultivate:** Develop a habit of studying the Bible to understand God's perspective on supernatural phenomena and spiritual warfare.
- **Equip:** Equip yourself with knowledge about the biblical teachings on angels, demons, and spiritual discernment to provide informed answers to questions about UFOs.
- **Engage:** Engage in conversations with fellow believers and non-believers about the biblical view of UFOs, offering a balanced and informed perspective.

Journaling Prompt

Reflect on your thoughts and feelings about the existence of UFOs and extraterrestrial life. How does understanding the biblical perspective on these phenomena influence your faith and approach to spiritual matters? Write about any experiences or questions you have related to this topic and how you can seek God's guidance in discerning the truth.

~

_____
_____
_____
_____
_____
_____
_____
_____
_____
_____
_____
_____
_____
_____
_____
_____
_____
_____
_____
_____
_____
_____
_____
_____
_____
_____
_____
_____

CHAPTER 8
TIME TRAVEL

Life can often feel overwhelming with its pressures and demands. Remember, no matter how challenging the situation, God is with you through every moment. His power and presence transcend time and space, offering guidance and comfort.

"Jesus Christ is the same yesterday and today and forever." - Hebrews 13:8 (NKJV)

The idea of time travel has always fascinated people, inspiring many science fiction stories. But is it really possible to travel into the past or future? We often think of time as a constant that governs everything we do, but modern science tells us that time is actually a variable.

We all "travel" through time from one moment to the next. But what if time could move differently? **Could there be places where time moves slower or faster?** Could time even stop or move in reverse? And what does the Bible say about this?

In the 4th century, Augustine suggested that time might be an illusion, but he was wrong because the Bible clearly tells us time has a beginning and an end. Sir Isaac Newton also believed time existed independently of everything else, but later he discovered he was mistaken.

Albert Einstein's theory of relativity showed that time and space are linked. He concluded that nothing could travel faster than the speed of light. According to his theory, the faster you travel, the slower you experience time. This was proven by an experiment with atomic clocks, where a clock on a jet lagged slightly behind a clock on the ground. **Time is not constant but relative to speed and gravity.**

Black holes, once thought to be theoretical, are now known to exist and have a gravitational pull that affects time. This suggests that gravity can be infinite, much like time and light. **This concept underscores the reality that God is an infinite being, the creator of infinite things.**

Muons are unstable subatomic particles that travel close to the speed of light and exist for only 2.2 microseconds. Yet, they penetrate the atmosphere and ground, showing that time is altered for them. This supports Einstein's theory of relativity.

Aerospace engineer Clyde McGee helped develop the GPS system, which relies on time-travel calculations. GPS satellites experience time differently due to their speed and distance from Earth. **Scientists correct these variations to ensure accuracy, proving that time variation is a real event.**

Observing distant stars and galaxies is like looking into the past because we see the light that traveled millions of years to reach us. This is not time travel but a simple observation of past events.

The Bible records visions of the future given to people like Daniel and John. These were prophetic visions, not actual time travel. **John's vision in Revelation was interactive, allowing him to see future events while still in the present.**

Scientifically, time travel as portrayed in fiction is impossible.

While time variation and alteration are real, humans cannot travel into the future or past. The Bible does not support the idea of changing historical events through time travel.

The Bible indicates that **God created time and can move within it**, but humans exist on a linear timeline. God knows the end from the beginning and can reveal the future to His prophets. **This proves that only God has foreknowledge of future events.**

Imagine watching a train from a helicopter; you can see the entire train at once. **Similarly, God sees all of time simultaneously**, while humans experience it moment by moment. This perspective helps us understand how God can know the future without affecting our free will.

Western culture views time as linear, but ancient Hebrew thought sees it as circular, continually moving upward toward God. This concept changes our understanding of the beginning and end of time.

Joshua 10 records a miraculous event where God stopped the sun to give Joshua more time to defeat his enemies. **This event shows God's power to alter time** and space, demonstrating that nothing is impossible for Him.

Philip was transported by the Spirit of the Lord to a different location in Acts 8. **This was a miraculous change of location, not time travel.** Miracles like this show that God's power transcends time and space.

I once experienced what seemed like time alteration when a long drive took significantly less time than it should have. **This was a supernatural event that allowed us to accomplish God's purpose.**

God's ability to predict future events with 100% accuracy shows that He has already seen the future. **He has foreknowledge, not fore-control**, and allows us to make our own choices. God is not restricted by time, but we are.

Ephesians 5:15-16 urges us to use our time wisely because the days are evil. **We must be led by the Spirit** to avoid time-wasting activities and focus on what God wants us to do. Time is valuable and should be used for God's purposes.

God, the Creator of time, is not bound by it. While humans are restricted by time, God can move within it as He pleases. The Bible does not address human time travel, but scientifically it remains impossible. **Our understanding of time should always consider God's infinite nature and His control over time.**

REFLECTIVE QUESTIONS

1. How does understanding that time is a variable, not a constant, change your perspective on daily life?
2. What can we learn from the biblical accounts of visions and miraculous events about God's control over time?
3. How does the concept of God knowing the end from the beginning influence your faith and trust in Him?
4. In what ways can you redeem the time in your daily activities to align more with God's purposes?
5. How can understanding God's infinite nature and control over time help you navigate challenges and uncertainties?

Actionable Steps

- **Cultivate** a deeper relationship with God by spending time in prayer and reading His Word, trusting in His control over time.
- **Equip** yourself with the knowledge of God's infinite

power and His ability to guide you through life, using
biblical examples and teachings.

- **Engage** with others by sharing the understanding of
  God's control over time and encouraging them to
  trust in His plan and purpose for their lives.

Journaling Prompt

Reflect on a time when you felt God's presence guiding you
through a challenging situation. How did this experience
strengthen your faith and trust in His control over time and
circumstances? Write about the ways you can apply this understanding to future challenges.

~

CHAPTER 9

ARTIFICIAL INTELLIGENCE AND THE COMING APOCALYPSE

As we navigate the complexities of technological advancements and their implications for our future, let us remember that our hope and security lie in the unchanging nature of God. No matter how advanced or threatening AI may seem, we can trust in God's sovereign plan and His promise to protect and guide His people.

"For God did not appoint us to wrath, but to obtain salvation through our Lord Jesus Christ." - 1 Thessalonians 5:9 (NKJV)

When I was young, technology was simple. We used clothespins and playing cards to make our bikes sound like motorcycles. Phones were party lines, and we could listen in on our neighbors. **Things have changed drastically.** Daniel's prophecy about knowledge increasing and people traveling extensively has come true in our time.

Human intelligence is a unique gift from God, unlike any other. **Our decisions are influenced** by relationships, educa-tion, emotions, and spiritual input. In contrast, artificial intelligence is programmed and lacks the depth and complexity of human reasoning and experience.

AI is essentially the ability of computer systems to mimic human behavior. This includes tasks like visual perception, speech recognition, decision-making, and language translation. What once was science fiction is now our reality.

Despite its advancements, **AI cannot match** the flexibility of human intelligence. It doesn't have the ability to develop "gut feelings" or hunches, and it remains limited to its programming. This limits its effectiveness in tasks that require everyday knowledge and nuanced reasoning.

AI lacks moral understanding until it is programmed. This raises the potential for misuse. For instance, Saudi Arabia granted citizenship to an AI named Sophia. This prompts questions about the future relationship between humans and AI, especially regarding rights and ethics.

There are experiments to implant AI chips in humans to store vast amounts of information. **This brings up concerns** about hacking and control. Could AI chips replace human teachers and control education? These are serious ethical and practical questions we need to consider.

Advanced AI could be used by the antichrist during the Great Tribulation. Technology itself is neutral, but its impact depends on who controls it. The internet, for example, can spread the gospel or facilitate evil acts. The value lies in the hands of its users.

The Bible warns about a mark required to buy or sell during the Great Tribulation. **AI could be used to implement** this mark, potentially enslaving people under the antichrist's rule. This concept, though futuristic, raises concerns about technology's role in future governance.

AI could create a lifelike image of the beast that speaks and demands worship. This image, empowered by AI, could deceive many during the Great Tribulation. The technology for such an image is already being developed, making this prophecy more plausible.

Despite the frightening prospects of AI and the coming tribulation, **Christians should not fear.** The church will be raptured before these events unfold. We should focus on strengthening our faith and sharing the gospel, knowing that our ultimate hope is in Jesus Christ.

REFLECTIVE QUESTIONS

1. **How has technology impacted your daily life and spiritual practices?** Think about how modern technology has affected your routines, communication, and faith journey. Consider both the positive and negative effects.

2. **In what ways do you see AI being used for good and for evil in today's world?** Identify examples of AI's beneficial uses and potential dangers. How do these examples align with the chapter's discussion on the moral neutrality of technology?

3. **What are your thoughts on the ethical implications of AI citizenship and rights?** Consider the implications of granting AI entities legal rights and citizenship. How does this challenge your understanding of humanity and personhood?

4. **How do you interpret the prophecy of the mark of the beast in relation to current technological advancements?** Reflect on the chapter's discussion about the mark of the beast and how modern technology could fulfill this prophecy. What are your

thoughts on the future intersection of faith and technology?

5. **How can you prepare spiritually for the events described in the chapter?** Think about the practical steps you can take to strengthen your faith and readiness for the end times. How can you use your understanding of prophecy to guide your actions and mindset?

Actionable Steps

- **Cultivate Awareness**: Stay informed about technological advancements and their potential ethical implications. Engage in discussions about AI and its impact on society, considering both the opportunities and risks.
- **Equip Your Faith**: Deepen your understanding of biblical prophecies and their relevance to modern times. Study scriptures related to the end times, and seek guidance from trusted spiritual leaders to strengthen your faith.
- **Engage in Evangelism**: Share the message of hope and salvation with others. Use technology responsibly to spread the gospel, leveraging social media, online platforms, and other tools to reach a wider audience.

Journaling Prompt

Reflect on your personal experiences with technology and AI. How have these advancements influenced your life and faith? Write about your thoughts on the ethical implications of AI and how you can prepare spiritually for the future. Consider the ways you can use technology to further your faith and share the message of the gospel.

～

_____
_____
_____
_____
_____
_____
_____
_____
_____
_____
_____
_____
_____
_____
_____
_____
_____
_____
_____
_____
_____
_____
_____
_____
_____
_____
_____
_____
_____

CHAPTER 10

TRANSHUMANISM, CRYONICS, AND ETERNAL LIFE

As we face the rapid advancements in technology and their potential impact on humanity, let us hold fast to the promises of God. True eternal life is found in Jesus Christ, not in technological innovations. Trust in His word and His plan for your life, knowing that He is the source of all true wisdom and life.

"He who believes in the Son has everlasting life; and he who does not believe the Son shall not see life, but the wrath of God abides on him." - John 3:36 (NKJV)

I grew up in Raytown, Missouri, and I loved following major league baseball, especially the Kansas City Athletics. One memorable event was when I saw Ted Williams play. Years later, after his death, his body was cryonically preserved. **Cryonics involves freezing bodies in hopes of future revival.** This practice leans toward the philosophy of transhumanism, which seeks to enhance human life and achieve immortality through technology.

Transhumanism is the idea of using technology to improve human life and even achieve eternal life. It aims to create a posthuman existence where people live forever and have enhanced cognitive abilities. This concept has ancient roots, like the quest for the fountain of youth. **The desire for eternal life is deeply embedded in human history and continues today.**

Some believe that human consciousness can be transferred to computers, a concept known as mind uploading. This raises questions about whether it enhances or diminishes human life. **Mind uploading is a controversial topic with both potential benefits and significant ethical concerns.**

CERN and Its Mysteries: CERN, the European Organization for Nuclear Research, operates the world's largest particle collider. **CERN's purpose is to advance human knowledge by exploring the fundamental particles of the universe**, but it is surrounded by mystery and conspiracy theories. Some fear the implications of its experiments, including the possibility of creating portals or other unknown phenomena.

Medical Implications of CERN: CERN has also made advances in medical technology, which can be beneficial. However, we must discern between technology that helps humanity and technology that tries to replace God. **Christians need to navigate the ethical implications of technological advancements carefully.**

Cryonics is the freezing of bodies with the hope of future revival. This process raises questions about life and death. **Cryonics challenges our understanding of when life ends and what it means to preserve it for future revival.**

Life and Death According to the Bible: The Bible provides clear answers about life and death. Life begins at conception and ends when the spirit departs the body. **Biblical teachings help us understand the true nature of life and death**, which differ from scientific and technological perspectives.

Despite the promises of cryonics, **science cannot create life.** No one knows if the science will ever exist that will allow a frozen body to be restored to life. **Human bodies are complex creations of God, and attempts to preserve them through freezing are unlikely to succeed.** The Bible teaches that life and death are in God's hands.

Eternal life is a gift from God, not something that can be achieved through technology. **Jesus promises eternal life to those who believe in Him.** Our hope for eternal life lies in the resurrection and the glorified bodies we will receive, not in technological advancements.

Salvation and eternal life come from believing in Jesus Christ. Confessing Jesus as Lord and believing in His resurrection is the path to true eternal life. **This promise is available to everyone who accepts Him.**

REFLECTIVE QUESTIONS

1. **How do you feel about the idea of transhumanism and using technology to enhance human life?** Reflect on the ethical implications and potential benefits and risks.

2. **What are your thoughts on cryonics and the attempt to freeze and revive human bodies?** Consider the scientific and spiritual perspectives on life and death.

3. **How does your faith influence your views on life, death, and the afterlife?** Think about how biblical teachings shape your understanding of these concepts.

4. **What is your understanding of mind uploading and its potential impact on humanity?** Reflect on

whether this could enhance or diminish what it means to be human.

5. **How can you navigate the advancements in technology while maintaining your faith and ethical standards?** Consider practical ways to engage with technology responsibly.

Actionable Steps

- **Cultivate Awareness:** Stay informed about advancements in technology, especially those related to transhumanism and cryonics. **Engage in discussions and research to understand the implications.**
- **Equip Your Faith:** Deepen your understanding of biblical teachings on life, death, and eternal life. **Study scriptures and seek guidance from spiritual leaders** to strengthen your faith and discernment.
- **Engage in Evangelism:** Share the message of eternal life through Jesus Christ. **Use technology responsibly to spread the gospel** and reach others with the hope of salvation.

Journaling Prompt

Reflect on your thoughts and feelings about transhumanism, cryonics, and the quest for eternal life. How do these concepts align with your faith and understanding of biblical teachings? Write about how you can navigate these technological advancements while maintaining your trust in God's plan for true eternal life.

CHAPTER II

FLAT EARTH THEORY

Understanding and wisdom are treasures that guide us towards truth. By seeking knowledge, we strengthen our minds and our faith. The search for truth, through science and spiritual reflection, enriches our lives and deepens our connection with God.

"The fear of the Lord is the beginning of wisdom, and the knowledge of the Holy One is understanding." - Proverbs 9:10 (NKJV)

Recently, there's been a comeback of the **flat earth theory**. This theory claims the earth is flat like a disc, not a round globe that spins. Even though there's plenty of evidence against it, this idea still fascinates some people.

Important figures like **Samuel Rowbotham and Lady Elizabeth Blount** were key to the flat earth movement. Rowbotham wrote "Zetetic Astronomy," and Blount started the Universal Zetetic Society, giving the movement a structured organization.

Wilbur Glenn Voliva, who founded a utopian community in Zion, Illinois, was a major flat earth supporter. He banned the teaching of a round earth in local schools and spread his beliefs through his radio station, even offering a reward to anyone who could prove the earth wasn't flat.

Early supporters of the **flat earth theory**, including some Christian leaders like E.W. Bullinger, misunderstood or misused scientific observations and biblical scriptures. They didn't have the modern scientific tools we have today, which led to these mistaken beliefs.

In 1956, Samuel Shenton started the **International Flat Earth Research Society**. This kept the flat earth theory going into the mid-20th century, even as scientific knowledge grew.

Some versions of the flat earth theory say the earth is surrounded by an **ice wall (Antarctica)** or is a square with four corners based on certain biblical interpretations.

A newer and more extreme version is the **holographic dome theory**. This idea suggests the universe is a holographic image inside a dome, making it seem like we live in a sophisticated computer simulation.

Both historical and modern **scientific evidence**, from Aristotle's time to today's space exploration, strongly refute the flat earth theory. Observations of stars and planets and photos from space show that the earth is a sphere.

Some flat earth believers think space agencies like **NASA are part of a global conspiracy**. They believe space images are fake and that the moon landings were staged.

Flat earth supporters often **misuse biblical scriptures** to support their claims. The Bible doesn't say the earth is flat or spherical. Christians are advised not to let this theory distract them from their faith.

REFLECTIVE QUESTIONS

1. What historical figures and societies contributed to the flat earth theory, and how did their beliefs shape public opinion?
2. In what ways did Wilbur Glenn Voliva influence the flat earth movement in the early 20th century?
3. How have advancements in science and technology challenged the flat earth theory?
4. What are some common conspiracy theories related to the flat earth belief, and why do they persist despite overwhelming evidence?
5. How should Christians approach the flat earth theory in light of their faith and scientific understanding?

Actionable Steps

- **Cultivate Critical Thinking**: Encourage yourself to think critically about information. Learn to tell the difference between credible sources and pseudoscience. Always question big claims and look for evidence.
- **Equip with Knowledge**: Get a good understanding of basic science, like how the earth moves and its shape. This knowledge helps you correct misconceptions and have informed discussions.
- **Engage in Constructive Dialogue**: Talk to others respectfully about the flat earth theory and other pseudoscientific beliefs. Share evidence and promote an open but critical approach to understanding the world.

Journaling Prompt

REFLECT ON A TIME when you encountered a widely held belief that you later discovered was false. How did this experience change your approach to evaluating new information? Write about the importance of seeking truth and the role of faith in guiding you through this process.

~

CHAPTER 12

GHOSTS

"Beloved, do not believe every spirit, but test the spirits, whether they are of God; because many false prophets have gone out into the world." —1 John 4:1 (NKJV)

A few years ago, my wife Loretta and I were traveling through Arkansas and needed a place to stay for the night. We stopped at a hotel in Eureka Springs. It was an older hotel, but it had been upgraded while keeping its quaint charm. After checking in and entering our room, I heard a commotion in the hallway. When I went to investigate, I found a camera crew and a journalist with a microphone. They told me they were from the Syfy Channel and were filming a documentary about the most haunted hotels in America. This hotel, they said, had once been a treatment facility for cancer and other ailments, and several people had mysteriously died there.

After we left the hotel, I did some research and discovered that it offered "ghost tours." This brings us to the questions: Do ghosts actually exist, and what does the Bible say about them?

First, let's define what we mean by the word ghosts. Today, a ghost is often thought of as a disembodied spirit, a slightly visible transparent image of a human who has lived and died, and for some reason is restricted to this physical earthly plane to complete a task or communicate a message to someone still living. **Biblically speaking, a ghost of this terminology does not exist.** However, ghost theorists often cite Matthew 14:26, where Jesus' disciples, seeing Him walking on the water, thought He was a ghost. Since Jesus did not rebuke them for saying they thought He was a ghost, many have used this scripture as proof that ghosts actually exist. But in the original Greek language of the New Testament, the word ghost and spirit are synonymous. The Greek word is "pneuma." That's why you'll find some versions of the Bible say the Holy Ghost while others say the Holy Spirit when talking about the third member of the Trinity.

"Now in the fourth watch of the night Jesus went to them, walking on the sea. And when the disciples saw Him walking on the sea, they were troubled, saying, 'It is a ghost!' And they cried out for fear. But immediately Jesus spoke to them, saying, 'Be of good cheer! It is I; do not be afraid.'" — Matthew 14:25-27

Angels are spirits, so it would have been appropriate for the disciples to think they saw an angelic being walking on the water, which could have brought them fear. That could be why Jesus did not rebuke them.

The Bible clearly tells us that when a person physically dies, **their spirit either goes to Hades or to Paradise**, also known as the Bosom of Abraham (Luke 16:22-23). Nowhere in the Bible does it say that the spirit of a human lingers on the earth.

Which brings another question: What is it that people see when they observe something they perceive to be a ghost? Obviously, they are seeing something, but what is it they are seeing? **Most likely they are seeing demonic beings who are on the earth** because they were cast down to the earth with Satan at his rebellion. There is also the possibility that a non-believer could see an angel of God and become fearful, perceiving it as a ghost due to their lack of spiritual discernment.

So why would the disciples be fearful if they saw an angel of God walking on the water? Why would they be afraid? Much like the shepherds were told not to be fearful when the angelic host appeared to them at the birth of Jesus, the disciples had to be told, "Do not be afraid." Why? Probably because of the overwhelming appearance and magnificence of the angels. But on the other hand, if they saw a demonic spirit (the spirit of a fallen angel), of course, they would be afraid. **Demonic spirits would be distorted and hideous and operate in the realm of fear.**

The bottom line is this: **Ghosts, as defined in current vernacular through theater, movies, and novels, do not exist.** But angels, both of God and fallen, do exist, and there are many biblical accounts of them being seen by natural eyes. Any time a spirit brings fear by appearing as a haunted or grotesque image, it is from the enemy and not of God. But it also is not a disembodied human spirit left wandering on the earth. **Beings appearing as ghosts are spirits, but not human spirits. Ghosts are NEVER human spirits.**

Christians are warned to NEVER participate in any activity, such as a séance, that would attempt to conjure up a spirit from the dead. Some do this as seemingly innocent entertainment, but it can bring deadly results.

INVITING DEMONS TO CHURCH

Many years ago, after attending a Christian university and majoring in theology, Loretta and I joined a small denominational church of about 300 members. Even though I was quite young at the time, I was asked to become the leader of the men's fellowship within the church. I was honored, so I accepted. I thought that I had been asked because of my vast knowledge of the Bible. After all, I had been a Bible student at a Christian university. However, I later found out that they had asked most of the men in the church, and they had all declined. I was their last resort. It was a humbling discovery.

Anyway, as director of the men's fellowship, I was automatically put on the church planning committee, and I anxiously awaited the first planning meeting. The meeting was in the basement of the parsonage. The committee consisted of the Women's Missionary Union leader, the Sunday School superintendent, the chairman of the board of deacons, the pastor's wife, and me. The pastor's wife was the committee chairman who opened the meeting by asking what progress had been made concerning the Halloween party for the youth of the church. Several suggestions were discussed, but after each suggestion, the pastor's wife would make the same comment, "Last year the party was so good. How can we top it this year?" It seemed as though every recommendation made did not measure up to the previous year's party.

Since this was my first committee meeting, I wanted to keep quiet, but my curiosity got the best of me. I asked, "What did the church do last year that is so difficult to top?"

The pastor's wife leaned over, placed her hand on my arm, and said, "Last year we got a large round table and brought it down here to the parsonage basement. We covered it with a white tablecloth, lit candles, brought in all the teenagers in the church, and had a séance. It was great!" I couldn't believe my ears. It was my first and my last committee meeting. How can we truly believe the Word of God and knowingly worship Satan? What an abomination! Apparently, some Christians see nothing wrong with Halloween parties in the church or allowing children to dress and imitate witches, vampires, and demonic beings. **Has the modern church become so humanistic that it sees nothing wrong with demon worship?** Children should be taught to imitate and emulate God, not the world of the occult.

"Beloved, do not imitate what is evil, but what is good. He who does good is of God, but he who does evil has not seen God." — 3 John 11

"Therefore be imitators of God as dear children." — Ephesians 5:1

SATANIC CON GAME

When people gather for a séance in order to speak to a departed person through a medium who is channeling their communication through a distorted voice, what is actually occurring? **The spirit and voice are not from a departed human. It is either from the trickery of man to deceive and manipulate the living, or it is demonic.** It is a type of satanic con game. The Bible teaches us that human spirits that have passed into Paradise or Hades are restricted and unable to communicate with the living (Luke 16:26).

What is a "familiar spirit"? **It is a demonic spirit that observes the living and has obtained knowledge that can be revealed or channeled through a witch or medium, giving the illusion that they are the spirit of someone who has died.** For this reason, the Bible says that contacting a medium to conjure up the dead is strictly forbidden, and the consequences of doing this were fatal. To speak to a familiar spirit that is pretending to be the spirit of someone departed brings confusion, deception, and destruction.

WHAT DOES THE BIBLE SAY ABOUT GHOSTS?

To become obsessed with ghosts and paranormal manifestations is another distraction from the enemy. For a Christian who is seeking answers from the spirit world, their only source should be the Holy Spirit, who will guide them in all truth and reveal things to come (John 16:13). A Christian should NEVER seek the kingdom of darkness for answers.

"Give no regard to mediums and familiar spirits; do not seek after them, to be defiled by them: I am the LORD your God." — Leviticus 19:31

"And the person who turns to mediums and familiar spirits, to prostitute himself with them, I will set My face against that person and cut him off from his people." — Leviticus 20:6

"So Saul died for his unfaithfulness which he had committed against the LORD, because he did not keep the word of the LORD, and also because he consulted a medium for guidance." —1 Chronicles 10:13

SHAPESHIFTERS

A favorite character in modern fantasy and science fiction movies is shapeshifters. The concept of shapeshifting is based on mythology, folklore, and speculative fiction. It is the ability to physically transform appearance into another being or object. These fictional beings can change their physical appearance so dramatically that they appear as completely different entities.

An example would be that a shapeshifter might appear as a bear, then moments later appear as a giraffe or a human. While these stories are drawn from fantasy, the question we may ask is: Is it a reality that a being can change its appearance and appear as something completely different from what it actually is?

Biblically speaking, there are beings recorded in the Bible that can change their appearance. We could call them a type of spiritual shapeshifter. While shapeshifters as portrayed in modern science fiction media are bizarre and extreme, it does reflect a spiritual truth that some spirit beings can change their appearance.

It's interesting that Satan himself has several different appearances described in Scripture. First, he was a cherub in heaven—powerful and beautiful (Ezekiel 28:14). After being expelled from heaven, he appeared as a serpent in the Garden of Eden when he spoke to Eve (Genesis 3:1). In the book of Revelation, it reveals that he was a dragon and a devil (Revelation 12:9). Second Corinthians 11:14 says that sometimes he even transforms himself into an angel of light. However, regardless of his appearance, he is still Satan and only appears to be something else.

Remember, Satan is a fallen angel, so if he has the ability to change his appearance, how much more is it possible for the angels of God (who obviously have greater power than fallen angels) to change their appearance? We know from Scripture that angels appeared in the heavens as glorious, heavenly beings when announcing the birth of Jesus to the shepherds. But as discussed earlier in this book, angels also appeared as men when they traveled to Lot's house in Sodom. But to the 185,000 Assyrians who were killed in one night by one angel, the angel must have appeared as a warrior (2 Kings 19:35).

When Jesus returns to catch away the church, Christians will go through a type of change as our resurrected bodies are transformed. At that point, in a moment, in the twinkling of an eye, we will be changed and receive our glorified bodies that are no longer restricted by the earthly rule of physics. This is a permanent change by God Himself and is not shapeshifting.

"In a moment, in the twinkling of an eye, at the last trumpet. For the trumpet will sound, and the dead will be raised incorruptible, and we shall be changed. For this corruptible must put on incorruption, and this mortal must put on immortality." — 1 Corinthians 15:52-53

The Bible teaches that at our transformation in the catching away of the church, we will be like Jesus is (1 John 3:2). We do not become gods, but we take our rightful place, which was God's intention from the beginning when He created us in His likeness and image. In Bible terms, we are transformed into the image of Christ (2 Corinthians 3:18).

DEMONIC POSSESSION IS NOT SHAPESHIFTING

When a person receives Jesus as their Lord and Savior and becomes "born again," the Holy Spirit (the Spirit of God Himself) moves inside of them to live permanently. Because of this, a demonic spirit cannot fully possess a Christian. Of course, evil spirits can torment and oppress a Christian who allows it, but they can never fully possess a Christian. The Bible says that God is light and in Him is no darkness (1 John 1:5). Christians cannot be possessed by a demon because the Holy Spirit already possesses them. However, non-believers living without the Holy Spirit can allow themselves to be fully possessed. When a demonic spirit fully possesses a person, they can literally change the physical features of that person. There have been times when a demon-possessed person was unrecognizable by their own family because their facial appearance had been so radically changed. Their strength can be increased way beyond normal.

Early in my ministry, I encountered a small, young demon-possessed girl that took six adult men to restrain, and they were extremely bruised when it was over. However, this is not shapeshifting; it is body modification and should not be confused with the shapeshifting concept. A grotesque demon-possessed person is still a person; they have not changed into another entity, their appearance was just altered. While fantasy stories of shapeshifters in literature and theater are fictitious, the concept of changing appearance does appear in Scripture.

However, even though the church will be transformed into glorified bodies, there is no evidence of humanity being able to change into another being. For humanity, shapeshifting must remain in the realm of folklore and science fiction. Mankind has never been, is not, and will never be shapeshifters.

REFLECTIVE QUESTIONS

1. **Why do you think people are fascinated by the idea of ghosts and haunted places?** Reflect on your own beliefs and experiences related to the supernatural.

2. **How does the biblical explanation of spirits differ from popular cultural views?** Consider how these differences affect your understanding of spiritual matters.

3. **What dangers does the Bible associate with engaging in practices like séances and consulting mediums?** Think about the spiritual implications and consequences of these actions.

4. **Why is it important for Christians to seek guidance solely from the Holy Spirit?** Reflect on times when you may have sought answers from questionable sources.

5. **How can believers cultivate discernment when encountering supernatural claims?** Identify ways to strengthen your spiritual discernment and reliance on God's Word.

- **Cultivate Awareness:** Educate yourself and others about the biblical stance on spirits and the dangers of engaging with the occult. Understanding the truth helps in avoiding deception.
- **Equip with Scripture:** Memorize and meditate on key Bible verses related to spiritual discernment and the Holy Spirit's guidance. This will equip you to respond biblically to supernatural claims.
- **Engage in Prayer:** Regularly pray for wisdom and discernment. Ask God to help you recognize and avoid any practices or beliefs that contradict His Word.

Journaling Prompt

Reflect on a time when you or someone you know encountered a supernatural experience. How did you respond, and how does this chapter influence your understanding of that event? Write about how you can apply biblical discernment in future situations involving spiritual claims.

$\sim$

_____
_____
_____
_____
_____
_____
_____
_____
_____
_____
_____
_____
_____
_____
_____
_____
_____
_____
_____
_____
_____
_____
_____
_____
_____
_____
_____
_____
_____
_____

GHOSTS

92

CHAPTER 13
THE MULTIVERSE AND ITS IMPLICATIONS

Trust in the unseen dimensions of God's power and love. Though
we may not fully comprehend the mysteries of the multiverse,
we can rest assured that God's presence permeates every realm,
guiding and protecting us.

**"While we do not look at the things which are seen, but at
the things which are not seen. For the things which are seen
are temporary, but the things which are not seen are
eternal." (2 Corinthians 4:18 NKJV)**

The term "multiverse" can mean different things
depending on who you ask. From a Christian point of
view, the heavens are thought to have multiple layers.
Paul talks about three heavens: the atmosphere around the
earth, the second heaven, and the third heaven, which is the
Paradise of God where the saints live until Jesus returns. The
ancient Book of Levi, found among the Dead Sea Scrolls,
mentions seven heavens. This shows that the idea of multiple

realms or dimensions has been around for a long time and has roots in ancient scripture.

Ephesians 4:10 tells us that Jesus ascended far above all the heavens, suggesting that the heavens have borders. **Psalm 113:4-6** also talks about an area above the heavens. This biblical insight hints that the universe might have limits and that the heavens could be dimensional rather than just vast expanses of space.

In the secular world, the multiverse is defined as the hypothetical set of all existing universes. These universes include everything—space, time, matter, information, and all physical laws. Within this multiverse are various types of universes like **parallel universes, flat universes, alternate universes, and multiple universes**, each with its own characteristics.

There are two main theories of the multiverse. The first theory suggests that multiple infinite universes exist simultaneously. This idea has been discussed since ancient Greek philosophy but remains unproven and paradoxical to many scientists. The second theory proposes that our universe consists of multiple dimensions. According to the Bible, this is not just a theory but a spiritual reality. **God and our existence with Him are multidimensional.**

The Bible clearly states in **2 Corinthians 4:18** that everything we see is made from what we don't see. **Mark 11:23** highlights that spoken words in the physical realm affect the spiritual realm. This supports the idea that our reality is **multidimensional, where the unseen influences the seen.**

1 Corinthians 2:9-10 tells us that unseen dimensions hold hidden mysteries revealed by the Holy Spirit. This means that spiritual insights and realities go beyond human understanding and are accessible through divine revelation.

Acts 19:11 recounts unusual miracles performed by Paul. Even today, in the Church Age, we can witness such miracles. These miraculous events come from the unseen spiritual realm, whether from the kingdom of light or darkness, and require spiritual discernment to understand.

I've had personal experiences and heard testimonies of miraculous events involving dimensional shifts. For instance, once a deer passed through my vehicle without causing any harm. Such occurrences suggest interactions between the **physical and spiritual dimensions.**

John 20:19 and John 20:26 describe Jesus entering a locked room after His resurrection. This indicates that physical laws were altered, or dimensional shifts occurred. This shows that divine interventions can transcend natural laws.

While the Bible doesn't mention multiple universes, it clearly speaks of multiple dimensions. Miracles on earth are manifestations of the **unseen dimension of heaven,** showcasing God's power over the physical world.

REFLECTIVE QUESTIONS

1. **How does the concept of multiple heavens in the Bible shape your understanding of the universe?** Reflect on how the idea of multilayered heavens influences your perception of the universe and your place in it.

2. **In what ways do you see the interaction between the physical and spiritual dimensions in your life?** Consider moments in your life where the spiritual realm may have influenced the physical world.

3. **What are some examples of unusual miracles you've experienced or heard about?** Think about miraculous events you've witnessed or learned about and their impact on your faith.

4. **How does the idea of dimensional shifts challenge or reinforce your faith?** Reflect on how understanding dimensional shifts influences your belief in God's power and presence.

5. **What steps can you take to cultivate spiritual discernment in recognizing the source of miracles?** Consider practical ways to develop discernment to understand the origin of miraculous events.

Actionable Steps

- **Cultivate:** Develop a habit of daily prayer and meditation, seeking the Holy Spirit's guidance to understand the mysteries of the unseen dimensions. Make it a priority to set aside time each day for prayer and meditation, asking for spiritual insight and understanding of the unseen world.

- **Equip:** Study biblical passages and scholarly interpretations that discuss the concept of multidimensional realities to deepen your theological knowledge. Invest time in reading the Bible and other theological works that explore the idea of multiple dimensions and their significance in Christian faith.

- **Engage:** Share your insights and experiences of the interaction between the physical and spiritual realms with your faith community to encourage collective growth. Actively participate in discussions and share your understanding of how the spiritual realm influences the physical world with others in your faith community.

JOURNALING **Prompt**

Reflect on a time when you experienced or witnessed an unusual event or miracle. How did it affect your understanding of God's presence and power in the unseen dimensions? Write about your thoughts and feelings, and how this experience has influenced your faith journey.

~

THE MULTIVERSE AND ITS IMPLICATIONS

_____
_____
_____
_____
_____
_____
_____
_____
_____
_____
_____
_____
_____
_____
_____
_____
_____
_____
_____
_____
_____
_____
_____
_____
_____
_____
_____
_____
_____
_____

CHAPTER 14
CLIMATE CHANGE

The Scriptures also say, "In the beginning, Lord, you were the one who laid the foundation of the earth and created the heavens. They will all disappear and wear out like clothes, but you will last forever. You will roll them up like a robe and change them like a garment. But you are always the same, and you will live forever." (Hebrews 1:10-12 CEV)

"While the earth remains, seedtime and harvest, cold and heat, summer and winter, day and night, shall not cease." (Genesis 8:22 ESV)

A big controversy today is the fear that human lifestyles are changing the climate so drastically that the earth will eventually become uninhabitable. Many believe the destruction caused by humans is happening so fast that the current generation might be the last to experience trees and green grass. This fear has been pushed so much that even things not connected to energy production or pollution, like bovine flatulence and coffee production, are being blamed for climate change. This mindset is often driven by fear and used politically to manipulate people. Fear is a destructive force that prevents rational thinking.

When I was young, I was taught that **climate change** was inevitable, but back then, we were warned about a coming ice age. Now, the same universities are teaching that the earth is warming and could become a desert. Throughout history, the earth's climate has changed dramatically, with periods much warmer or colder than today. The study of ancient climate, or paleoclimatology, shows that **climate change is not a new phenomenon.**

In ancient Egypt and Mesopotamia, prolonged droughts and floods caused climate changes. In the 17th century, Robert Hooke theorized that fossils of giant turtles in England indicated a much warmer climate in the past, possibly due to the earth shifting on its axis. Others believed these fossils resulted from Noah's flood. In the 19th century, astronomer Heinrich Schwabe studied how the sun affected the earth's climate, contributing to the field of paleoclimatology.

A few decades ago, a radical movement saw protestors throwing paint on SUVs because they believed these vehicles consumed more fuel. Animal activists did the same to fur coats, even though many were synthetic. These protests, driven by misinformed fear, eventually faded away.

Presidential candidate Al Gore once claimed there was a 75% chance the Arctic ice cap would be ice-free within five to seven years, which never happened. This prediction, now seen as humorous, is an example of the fate of climate change hysteria.

What Does the Bible Say About Climate Change? When Jesus returns, people will be living normal lives (Matthew 24:37-39). Genesis 8:22 reassures us that the earth will have continuous seasons. **Seedtime and harvest will continue**, and there will be a balance between cold and heat while the earth remains, meaning there is no need to panic about the earth being destroyed by mankind before Jesus returns.

After Jesus sets up His kingdom, the earth will continue for another thousand years (during His millennial reign) with seed-time and harvest, cold and heat, summer and winter, and day and night. After this period, there will be a great judgment, and God will eradicate all evil. Revelation 21:1 describes a new heaven and earth, meaning a refurbished earth, as the Greek word "kainos" indicates.

Peter says the earth will be reserved for fire (2 Peter 3:7). This means God will cleanse the earth, creating a renewed earth and atmosphere after the final judgment. Death will no longer be a factor for those living on the new earth, and God will live with mankind for eternity (Revelation 21:3-4).

Should we be concerned about the condition of the earth? Yes, we should minimize pollutants and take care of the environment (Genesis 2:15). However, we should not let fear drive us to make irrational decisions that restrict us from living the abundant life promised by God (John 10:10).

Reflective Questions

1. **How does the Bible's assurance of continuous seasons affect your view on climate change?** Reflect on the stability promised in Genesis 8:22 and how it influences your thoughts on current climate concerns.

2. **What are some ways you can balance environmental responsibility without succumbing to fear?** Consider practical steps to care for the earth while trusting in God's control over its future.

3. **How do historical climate changes influence your understanding of today's climate discussions?** Think about how past climate events shape your perspective on modern climate change debates.

4. **In what ways can fear about the future impact rational decision-making?** Reflect on how fear has influenced your choices and how faith can guide you towards sound decisions.

5. **How can you cultivate a biblical perspective on environmental stewardship in your daily life?** Consider ways to incorporate Scripture's teachings into your approach to caring for the environment.

Actionable Steps

- **Cultivate:** Develop a habit of daily prayer and meditation, seeking God's guidance to understand His control over the earth's future. Make it a priority to set aside time each day for prayer and meditation, asking for peace and wisdom in your environmental responsibilities.

- **Equip:** Study biblical passages and scholarly interpretations that discuss God's plan for the earth to deepen your theological knowledge. Invest time in reading the Bible and other resources that explore the balance between environmental care and trust in God's sovereignty.

- **Engage:** Share your insights and experiences on environmental stewardship with your faith community to encourage collective growth. Actively participate in discussions and share your understanding of how to care for the earth in a way that honors God's promises.

Journaling Prompt

Reflect on a time when you felt fear about the future of the earth. How did this fear impact your decisions and actions? Write about how trusting in God's control over the earth's future can change your perspective and influence your approach to environmental stewardship.

~

HIDDEN MYSTERIES AND THE BIBLE OFFICIAL WORKBOOK

_____
_____
_____
_____
_____
_____
_____
_____
_____
_____
_____
_____
_____
_____
_____
_____
_____
_____
_____
_____
_____
_____
_____
_____
_____
_____
_____
_____

CHAPTER 15

HEAVEN, HELL, AND ETERNITY

"Let not your heart be troubled; you believe in God, believe also in Me. In My Father's house are many mansions; if it were not so, I would have told you. I go to prepare a place for you." - John 14:1-2 (NKJV)

I n this chapter, I want to share my thoughts on heaven, hell, and eternity as described in the Bible. Many religions have their own versions of a peaceful, eternal place. For example, Hindus call it "Svarga," Buddhists call it "Sagga," and Muslims call it "Jannah." The ancient Canaanites believed in the land of Mot, while Christians and Jews simply refer to it as heaven.

Heaven in Christianity is not just an idea; it is a real place. According to the Christian Bible, heaven's beauty is beyond human description. Genesis 1:1 tells us about the creation of multiple heavens, indicating a multi-dimensional realm. The Hebrew word for heaven is plural, which shows that there are different areas and dimensions within heaven. The Apostle Paul mentioned visiting the third heaven, while other texts, such as the Testament of Levi, suggest there are seven heavens.

Within these heavens, there is the holy city known as the **Heavenly Jerusalem**. This city is separate yet connected to the earthly Jerusalem, forming what is referred to as Yerushalayim. The Bible describes a time when the **New Jerusalem** will descend from heaven after the millennium and merge with the earthly Jerusalem. This city will be the eternal home of God's saints. The New Jerusalem's size is staggering, with each side measuring 1,500 miles in length, width, and height, extending far beyond our atmosphere.

Heaven is vast, but it has **boundaries**. Ephesians 4:10 tells us that Jesus ascended far above all the heavens, indicating that there is a realm beyond the known heavens that encapsulates God's glory. **Angels** play a significant role in the interaction between heaven and earth. Biblical accounts, such as Jacob's vision of a ladder and various angelic visitations, suggest that angels move between these realms through portals.

Hell is described using three Greek words: Hades, Gehenna, and Tartarus. Each term highlights different aspects of torment and punishment after death. Hades refers to the abode of the dead, Gehenna is associated with divine punishment, and Tartarus is described as a deep abyss for the wicked. Hell was originally created for Satan and his angels but is also for those who reject Jesus Christ.

We all have an **eternal destiny**. Humans are eternal beings with a beginning but no end. Our eternal destination—whether heaven or hell—is determined by our relationship with Jesus Christ during our earthly lives. This choice is crucial and has eternal consequences.

Reflect on these key points and consider how they shape your understanding of eternity. Ask yourself what the multidimensional aspect of heaven means to you, how the description of the New Jerusalem impacts your view of God's promises, and how the reality of hell influences your sense of urgency in sharing the gospel.

Take actionable steps to **cultivate** a deeper understanding of these concepts by studying relevant scriptures. **Equip** yourself with knowledge about hell to inform your discussions about salvation. **Engage** in practices that align with your eternal destiny, such as prayer, worship, and acts of service.

Remember the words of encouragement from John 14:1-2, where Jesus promises to prepare a place for us in His Father's house. This promise should fill us with hope and strengthen our faith as we look forward to our eternal home.

REFLECTIVE QUESTIONS

1. **What is the significance of the Bible describing heaven as a multi-dimensional realm?** How does this understanding of heaven shape your view of the afterlife and its complexities?

2. **How does the description of the New Jerusalem impact your perception of heaven?** Think about what the immense size and beauty of the New Jerusalem suggest about God's plan for His people.

3. **Why is the concept of angelic portals important in understanding the interaction between heaven and earth?** Consider the role of angels and how their interactions reflect God's ongoing involvement in our lives.

4. **What are the implications of hell being a real place of eternal punishment?** Reflect on how this understanding of hell influences your sense of

urgency in sharing the gospel and living a righteous life.

5. **How does the concept of eternity influence your daily life and decisions?** Think about how the promise of eternal life with God shapes your priorities, actions, and outlook on life.

Actionable Steps

- **Cultivate** a deeper understanding of biblical descriptions of heaven. Study scriptures like Genesis 1:1 and Revelation 21. Reflect on how these descriptions impact your faith and understanding of God's promises.
- **Equip** yourself with knowledge about the reality and purpose of hell by reading passages such as Matthew 25:41, Revelation 20:10, and Luke 16:24-25. Use this understanding to inform discussions about salvation with others.
- **Engage** in daily practices that align with your eternal destiny. Spend time in prayer, worship, and acts of service, keeping in mind the eternal significance of your relationship with Jesus Christ.

Journaling Prompt

Reflect on the concept of eternity and write about how the promise of eternal life in the New Jerusalem influences your daily decisions and outlook on life. Consider how this perspective shapes your priorities and interactions with others.

_____
_____
_____
_____
_____
_____
_____
_____
_____
_____
_____
_____
_____
_____
_____
_____
_____
_____
_____
_____
_____
_____
_____
_____
_____
_____
_____
_____
_____
_____
_____
_____

_____
_____
_____
_____
_____
_____
_____
_____
_____
_____
_____
_____
_____
_____
_____
_____
_____
_____
_____
_____
_____
_____
_____
_____
_____
_____
_____
_____
_____
_____

CHAPTER 16

THE MYSTERY OF THE HEBREW LANGUAGE

"Heaven and earth will pass away, but My words will by no means pass away." - Matthew 24:35 (NKJV)

The Bible is a prophetic book, revealing God's plan from beginning to end. **Every word contains revelation** since the Bible is the inspired Word of God. Though it's full of mysteries, these are meant to be revealed to Christians. The Hebrew language, which God used to write the Ten Commandments, is unique and different from any other language. It's the same language Jesus used when He spoke to Saul on the road to Damascus.

The Hebrew language is special, with ancient sages and rabbis talking about 70 layers or dimensions to each of its 22 letters. Each letter has a color, frequency, numeric value, and a symbol. For example, the symbol for Dalet, the fourth letter, is a door. **Hebrew is encoded with divine messages**, proving it's not just inspired but also crafted with precision only God could achieve.

The Hebrew language was given to us 3,500 years ago with

2.5 million words. Even words like the Hebrew term for "computer" existed back then, even though their full meanings were unknown. This shows the spiritual principle of speaking the word before seeing its manifestation.

- **Analog vs. Digital**: Most world languages are like analog recordings, but Hebrew is like a digital recording. Digital files can be copied without losing quality, while analog files degrade over time. Hebrew remains unchanging and eternal, unlike languages such as English, which evolve over time. For example, the King James Bible from 1611 used different spellings and had only 24 letters in the alphabet.

When copying the Torah, a Hebrew scribe must be precise, using mathematical formulas where even a small mistake requires starting over. **Scribes must take a ceremonial bath** before writing the name of God each time. This meticulous process has kept God's Word unaltered through centuries.

- **The Ezekiel Stones**: On one trip to Israel, I saw the Ezekiel Stones, flat square stones found in Ezekiel's tomb near Baghdad. The stones have the entire book of Ezekiel written on them. Unlike modern Bibles, which say "There was a king," these stones say "There is a king," showing a present tense perspective, indicating the king was alive when the stones were written. The letters on these stones are in relief, not carved in, which remains a mystery to archaeologists.

- **Music from God**: Hebrew is also musical. Each letter has a frequency, and a professor once fed the Hebrew letters of Psalm 23 into a computer, which then produced beautiful music. King David played his harp for King Saul, and the demons tormenting Saul left. David's music may have literally played words containing the power to repel evil spirits. **Psalm 119 is a unique psalm**, divided into 22 stanzas, each corresponding to a letter in the Hebrew alphabet, showing God's special connection to Hebrew.

- **Queen Esther's Prophecy Fulfilled**: Many hidden codes exist within the Hebrew Bible, revealing prophecies once events unfold. For example, Queen Esther's strange request to hang Haman's already dead sons was seen as a prophecy. In 1946, 10 Nazi war criminals were hanged, fulfilling Esther's prophecy. The Jews celebrate this victory during Purim, and many Nazi attacks on Jews coincided with this holiday.

- **The Aleph and the Tav**: Jesus refers to Himself as the Alpha and Omega, but in Hebrew, it's the Aleph and the Tav, the first and last letters of the Hebrew alphabet. This untranslatable word from Genesis 1:1 means Jesus was there in the beginning with God, creating everything. **John 1:1 confirms Jesus as the Word**, existing with God from the start, and through Him, all things were made.

*In the beginning was the Word, and the Word was
with God, and the Word was God. All things were
made through Him, and without Him nothing
was made that was made.*

—JOHN 1:1-3 (NKJV)

Jesus is not just letters in an alphabet but the Word of God
from the beginning. The end will come when God's plan is
complete, redeeming His creation to partake in eternal life.

REFLECTIVE QUESTIONS

1. **What does the uniqueness of the Hebrew
   language reveal about God's communication with
   us?** Reflect on how understanding Hebrew's
   complexity enhances your appreciation of the Bible.
2. **How does knowing the Hebrew language is
   digital-like and unchanging impact your view of
   Scripture?** Consider the significance of a language
   that remains precise and unaltered over thousands of
   years.
3. **Why is it important that scribes have maintained
   such precision in copying the Torah?** Think about
   the dedication required and what it means for the
   accuracy of the Bible we have today.
4. **What can we learn from Queen Esther's prophecy
   and its fulfillment?** Reflect on how prophecies, even
   those hidden in codes, demonstrate God's control
   over history.
5. **How does the Aleph and the Tav deepen your
   understanding of Jesus as the Word?** Consider the

significance of Jesus being present from the beginning and what that means for His role in creation and salvation.

Actionable Steps

- **Cultivate** a deeper understanding of the Hebrew language and its significance by studying the original Hebrew text of key Bible passages. Reflect on the hidden layers and meanings within the language.
- **Equip** yourself with knowledge about the preservation of the Hebrew Scriptures. Learn about the meticulous work of scribes and the historical artifacts like the Ezekiel Stones to appreciate the accuracy of God's Word.
- **Engage** in sharing the profound aspects of the Hebrew language and its prophecies with others. Use this knowledge to strengthen your faith and the faith of those around you, highlighting the divine inspiration and precision of the Bible.

Journaling Prompt

Reflect on the mysteries of the Hebrew language and how it enhances your understanding of God's Word. Write about how this knowledge influences your faith and your relationship with Scripture. Consider what new insights you have gained and how they shape your view of the Bible's divine inspiration.

Harrison House is a Spirit-filled, Word of Faith Christian publisher dedicated to spreading the message of faith, hope, and love through our wide range of inspiring publications. Committed to the messages that highlight the power of the Word and Spirit, we provide books, devotionals, and study guides that empower believers to live victorious, faith-filled lives.

Our resources are designed to help readers grow spiritually, strengthen their faith, and experience the transformative power of God's Word. Harrison House is passionate about equipping Christians with the tools they need to fulfill their divine purpose and impact the world for Christ.